NEW *FASHION*
Dopress Books
ILLUSTRATION

CYPI PRESS

Preface

Carmen Dell'Orefice once said, "I've witnessed the wax and wane of fashion illustrations. But what keeps me excited is it never truly fades away. It always comes back, just like a sweet old melody."

A hundred years ago, fashion illustrations were the heart and soul of fashion magazines. In earlier editions of *Harper's Bazaar* and *Vogue* magazines, fashion illustrations were abundant from cover to cover with fearless, unique and original fashion styles that sparked new and exciting thoughts for the readers. However, it was René Gruau, a French master illustrator, who became the epitome of fashion illustration. His illustrations worked in close ties with "New Look", a series of style lines launched by Dior in the 1950s. He brought high-couture French fashion to the public with his fluid use of lines and large areas of color. His business bond with Dior achieved immense success with designers, models and fans alike, and his work is still unparalleled in the fashion industry today.

Nevertheless, during the late 20th century, fashion illustration was overshadowed by fashion photography. Famed for its exact texture of light and shadow and the convenience of fast copy, fashion photography replaced the dominating role of fashion illustration and appealed to the idea of full expression in the always-emerging photographs with inexhaustible splendor and styles.

Fortunately, for the never-ending fashion circle, which never ceases its pursuit of perfection, a good piece of fashion illustration is still considered as good, if not better than an ordinary photograph. This theory is eloquently illustrated with the works of David Downton. Compared to photographs, which can be more monotonous, works hand-drawn by illustrators bear more artistic virtuosity and personal touch. Today, the art of fashion illustration is reviving and requested by many top brands and labels. Modern illustrations take in digital techniques and have also set a trend and contributed artistically within the fashion circle.

This book comes to fruition by encompassing the collective works of 24 eminent fashion illustrators from across the world. It offers the most chic and modern fashion designs with an innovative interpretation of fashion through the form of illustrations.

CONT

Sara Vera Lecaro	006	056 Masaki Mizuno
Choonfai	012	062 Cecilia Carlstedt
Pippa McManus	020	070 Raphaël Vicenzi
Floyd Grey	030	078 Shinn Wen
Andriana Chunis	036	086 David Despau
Anne Cresci	042	094 Gabriel Villena

Ëlodie	098	142	Nicole Jarecz
Katrinn Pelletier	106	150	Sandra Suy
Lutheen	114	156	Silke Werzinger
Ko. Machiyama	122	168	Stina Persson
Mamzelle Poppy	128	176	Svetlana Makarova
Natalia Sanabria	134	184	Yana Moskaluk

Sara Vera Lecaro

Sara Vera Lecaro is an art director and fashion illustrator based in Ecuador. Her talent as a potential artist was noticed since she was a little girl. Her works have been posted in magazines, blogs and expositions in several countries such as Ecuador, Argentina, Colombia, México and France. She won the best Ecuadorian Illustration Portfolio in the Behance Portfolio Review 2013. In addition, Sara was invited to be part of the jury in the illustration field for the 2014 and 2015 Portfolio Reviews in her country.
Her inspirations come from fashion, fairy tales, history and art.

Tools and materials: Mixed artwork, traditional drawing, watercolor, markers and digital painting

- **How did you get in touch with fashion illustration and what's your understanding of this form of art?**

Actually I'm taking a master's course in Fashion Design, and now I understand, it's not just about drawing pretty pictures but communicating what the designer wants to say. Your illustration is a reflection of their inspiration, and when done successfully your illustration style becomes your trademark.

- **What's the concept of your art creation?**

My concept is basically about fashion and my inspiration is based on fashion icons, fairy tales and history books. I usually try with watercolors and textures, but recently I´m just playing with digital techniques.

- **Who is your most admired fashion artist?**

Fashion is another way to express our emotions and inspirations as contemporary artists, and if I have to compare that phrase with someone really close and big in fashion history it would be Alexander McQueen and Elsa Schiaparelli – they inspire me in fashion and the way they perceived the world.

- **How do you understand the combination of these two fields – fashion and illustration art?**

For me, art is a very extensive word. Through fashion, we find a way to express ourselves and find inspiration. It's art, too, and so is illustration. I love to mix things together and get inspired by them. Fashion and illustration work perfectly together, like a canvas for a masterpiece.

1
Vintage Twins 02

1
Aviso Fabri
2
Gbss16final

1
Revista
2
DB2
3
Queen Valentino

Choonfai

Choonfai is an illustrator based in Singapore, mainly working with advertising agencies to create commercial illustrations and his own artworks. His other passions include art, fashion, music, life, travel and nature; he finds inspiration in his surroundings. His illustration style denotes elegance, hints of mystery and a contemporary aesthetic that tells stories in a whispering tone.

Tools and materials: Digital painting

■ How did you get in touch with fashion illustration?

I studied communication art and majored in illustration, but not fashion illustration in particular. I've always been fascinated by fashion so fashion illustration came naturally to me when I started creating.

■ Where do you find your inspiration?

Inspiration comes in many different ways and forms, from random images, my old travel photos, old stories at the back of my mind, etc. I first think of a storyline and then the rest just falls into place.

■ In terms of creation techniques, in which aspect do you think you distinguish from other fashion illustrators?

I invent my own characters when I create the illustrations instead of relying on photos of models, so the faces in my works are quite distinguishable.

■ What do you think about the advantage of fashion design in the form of illustration?

When fashion is shown in the form of illustration, it is depicted in a highly imaginative world that has no limitations; it's not limited by the model wearing it, the lights landed on it, not even the material and texture of the garment itself. It captivates the viewers in a completely different way than other media.

1
Melting Beauty

1
Awakening of the Puppresses 03
2
Awakening of the Puppresses 02
3
Awakening of the Puppresses 05

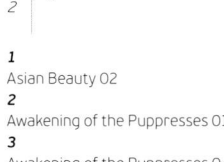

1
Asian Beauty 02
2
Awakening of the Puppresses 01
3
Awakening of the Puppresses 04

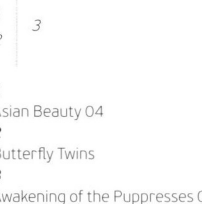

1
Asian Beauty 04
2
Butterfly Twins
3
Awakening of the Puppresses 06

Pippa McManus

After working professionally in the past twelve years, Pippa McManus has emerged as one of Australia's best-known fashion illustrators. Her fashion obsession has taken her from Los Angeles to collaborate with Aurelio Costarella for NY Fashion Week and many other fashion companies. She has travelled to Sydney, Australia to illustrate MBFWA and on to Paris and London for Mary Katrantzou and other designers and brands such as Dolce & Gabbana, and Australia's Aurelio Costarella, Ellery, and Manning Cartell. After several sell-out exhibitions over the past five years, Pippa is now focusing solely on her fine art fashion illustrations that are displayed in galleries nationally and internationally.

Tools and materials: Acrylic paint, charcoal, soft pastel, paint pens and spray paint

■ What's the concept of your art creation?

My design concept is as simple as just wanting to draw the most beautiful girls in the world. I always say, "I paint the clothes I want to wear and the girls I want to be." I love the process of painting a beautiful female face, using washes of only black acrylic paint and adding charcoal to deepen areas of shadow. I leave the color for the background and especially the clothing, which is intended to be the more vibrant part of the image.

■ Who is your most admired fashion artist?

I try not to look at other fashion illustrators' works so as not to be much influenced by them. I prefer to look at the models and the catwalk. It's the fashion part that I find inspiring and it always dictates what direction the painting will go. I also like to mix in traditional costume or sewing techniques that I see. Usually if something pops up visually on my radar quite a few times, it ends up making its way into a painting.

■ How do you understand the combination of these two fields – fashion and illustration art?

I think fashion and illustration blend beautifully because they are both fast-paced vocations. Fashion designers are under pressure to create art that changes every six months (or less now!) and illustrators work quickly and deliberately unlike fine artists who conceptualise and actualise their works over a longer period of time.

■ How does the knowledge of fashion effect your illustration art?

Having some knowledge of sewing, pattern-making and print-making is extremely helpful to me as a fashion illustrator. I studied fashion design for three years in college and use that insight almost subconsciously when painting.

1
Indian Summer

1 Anna Rosa
2 Winterfell

1 Divine Idol
2 McQueen My Queen

1
Bohemian Rhapsody
2
The French Queen
3
Devon Dreams
4
Miami Lights
5
Barbara's Bunch

1 N is for Nimue
2 Roses & Rosary

Floyd Grey

Floyd Grey is from Kuala Lumpur, Malaysia. He works full time as a digital imaging artist, fashion illustrator and photographer. Floyd has a love for indie folk music and is very intrigued by the fashion icon Marilyn Monroe, and the nostalgic qualities black and white play in fashion and photography.

Tools and materials: Photoshop and Wacom Tablet

- What's the concept of your art creation?

My design concept is about reality and idealism. I escape from the real world and live in my small ideal world.

- Who is your most admired fashion artist?

David Downton and René Gruau. I love the simplicity and minimal yet dramatic brush strokes and color combinations of their works.

- How do you understand the combination of these two fields – fashion and illustration art?

Fashion is about clothing, and illustration captures something amazing by using hand-drawings or digital techniques. The combination of these two fields is full of interest.

- What do you think about the advantage of fashion design in the form of illustration?

It helps make the vision of the designer and creates a more easily understandable design.

1
Frida
2
Kate Moss

	1	
2	3	4

1
Man in White Suit
2
Black and White Woman
3
Constance
4
Hilary

Andriana Chunis

Andriana Chunis is a designer and illustrator based in her home city Lviv, Ukraine. Her illustrations are personal projects as well as commercial works for clients. After graduation, Andriana searched for "her way" through various areas of design. Her journey came full circle when she chose her original love, drawing illustration, utilizing line, shape and texture to emphasize the important elements in her illustrations.

Tools and materials: Photoshop drawing, hand drawing and textures

- **What's the concept of your art creation?**

When it comes to my work I have one rule – to emphasize the spark, the inspiration behind my work. I try to create certain moods in each of my works so that it can draw people in to create their own feelings about it. This is what I like the most.

- **Who is your most admired fashion artist?**

I get inspired by the works of Gill Button, Cecilia Carlstedt, Daniel Egneus, and Dadu Shin. They are the fashion artists I really admire.

- **Would you please give us a brief introduction about the history of fashion illustration?**

The history of fashion illustration dates back to the 16th century, when the etching process was used to create images. It took skilled artists of that period to produce the image. Since then, fashion illustrations have developed, as artworks aside from the finished product of fashion design. Fashion illustrations were ubiquitous until the 1920s. With the invention of the camera, fashion ideas could be communicated much faster through photography.

- **What do you think of the current forms of expression for fashion illustration? For future creations, in which aspect do you expect to make breakthroughs?**

I think a kind of revival is taking place with fashion illustration. More magazines, blogs and publishing houses are using fashion illustration alongside photography. Although it is not new, fashion illustration has a retro feel about it and that is very popular right now. Hand illustration can capture different accents on a particular style and create moods and aesthetics that a camera cannot.

1

1
Black Coat

1	3
2	

1
Street Chinese
2
4
3
Winter Set

1
Streer Girls
2
Street Chinese 03
3
Yellow

041

Anne Cresci

Anne Cresci graduated from Ecole Emile Cohl in Lyon, France in 1999. Since then she has worked as an editor for fashion and lifestyle magazines, as well as children's books all over the world. Her works were included in *Cosmopolitan*, *Marie Claire*, *Be* magazine, *Glamour*, *Votre Beauté* magazine, etc. Anne is a mother of two kids, two cats and a rabbit and resides in Lyon. Anne's work is mostly digital with vibrant watercolor splashes, feminine and bright, full of details and highly inspired by nature. She likes to mix detailed faces and characters with flowers and animals usually inspired by childhood fairytales and fashion and has a passion for patterns.

Tools and materials: Digital painting and watercolor

- **How did you get in touch with fashion illustration?**

I drifted toward fashion illustration quite naturally. I've always said I admired fashion illustrators, and I'm crazy about clothes, so I guess it was inevitable!

- **Where do you find your inspiration?**

Most of the time I read fashion and life style magazines, and honestly, Internet is just the biggest stock of images you can imagine! For example, I spend a huge amount of time on Pinterest, a social network for creative minds. I also just recently discovered Instagram. I know I'm a bit late but better late than never! When I have my mind full of animals, landscapes, dresses and beautiful women I do a mix of them all and add sweet touches of color.

- **In terms of creation techniques, in which aspect do you think you distinguish from other fashion illustrators?**

It's hard to answer that because I'm not sure if my work is driven by my intellect. I'm more about feelings and general pictures. I go with my instinct and trust my gut intuition at the moment I'm doing it. So I guess that my personality tends to get through but not in a controlled way.

- **What do you think of the current forms of expression for fashion illustration? For future creations, in which aspect do you expect to make breakthroughs?**

I'm in awe of all the very realistic drawings. It's really fascinating for me to see how an illustrator can be so close to reality. But what touches me most is when some movement and offtrack detail is added to the illustration, when it's not quite finished, and a bit messy. I can see many very talented people out there! In the future I will try to come up with a more personal vision of fashion and lifestyle illustration. And definitely I will try to find the time to experiment more! The last years have been quite intense so I think I need a little time to feed my creativity and find my own way of interpretation.

1
Blonde 02

1
2 3

1
Verseau
2
Topshop Tatto
3
Marie Claire Hors Series

1
Cosmopolitan Munich
2
Vierge

1
Glamour Espagne
2
Company Magazine

1 Lion
2 Balance

053

1 *2*

1
Flora
2
Endless Jewelry

Masaki Mizuno

Masaki Mizuno was influenced greatly during his childhood by his mother, a painter. Later he immersed himself in drawing illustrations independently while attending a fashion college. After graduaton, he spent seven years exploring pure art, a period of his life which has a tremendous influence on the way he illustrates fashion today.

Tools and materials: Analogue, hand painting with acrylic, air brush and rollers

- **What's the concept of your art creation?**

Upon creating my fashion illustrations, I utilize the theme of Eros. I think it is essential to display the beauty of fashion's silhouette and details through the overall balance of the figure, pose and angle as well. Therefore I do not have a specific image of a model in mind. Focusing on the depiction of the clothing's design and charm, I prefer to use expressionless faces, an unnatural impression.

- **Where do you find your inspiration?**

I obtain inspiration from history, daily life, and various places. It doesn't come from something fixed, and communication with other people sometimes also triggers certain images.

- **What do you think about the advantage of fashion design in the form of illustration?**

I believe it's possible to elevate the realm of fashion into art. There are different elements or ways to capture style. In my case, I think it is possible to change the artistic value of trend-driven fashion through one single tableau or illustration.

- **What do you think of the current forms of expression for fashion illustration? For future creations, in which aspect do you expect to make breakthroughs?**

I can sense that the development of digital graphics has produced many great works, which can be seen on the Internet. However on the other hand, I sense that this development has also decreased the market demand for analogue, hand-painted style of work. My goal is to create pieces that go beyond the field of illustration; work that could also be considered in the realm of pure art.

1

1
Alexander McQueen 2009

1
Givenchy 2009
2
Jean Paul Gaultier 01
3
Jean Paul Gaultier 02

1	2	5
3	4	6

1
Emporio Armani 2014
2
Flower Shirt 2010
3
Comme des Garcons Paper Dress
4
5351 Pour Les Femmes
5
Fendi 2014
6
Dolce & Gabbana 2014

Cecilia Carlstedt

Even from an early age, drawing and painting has been Cecilia Carlstedt's favorite medium. After finishing her formal studies at the Stockholm University majoring in History of Art she continued with a foundation and B.A. in Graphic design and Illustration at the London College of Communication, which also included a semester abroad at the Fashion Institute of Tehnology in New York. After graduaton in 2003 she began her career as an illustrator, and has been commissioned for a wide range of clients such as Nina Ricci, H&M, Vogue, LMVH, J. Lindeberg, Lancome and Show Studio.

Tools and materials: Mixed media on paper, including ink, pencil and collage

- How did you get in touch with fashion illustration?

I was always drawing as a child. My subjects could be anything really, but I remember distinctly one time in my early teens when I came across a fashion illustration in a magazine and it just blew my mind. I really had no special interest in clothes or fashion, but this fast ink drawing really made an impression on me and was a starting point to a growing interest in fashion illustration. I have never had a wish to become a fashion designer myself, and it has always been the interpretation of fashion that has interested me. I have studied art and graphic design, but my formal education never involved fashion illustration specifically, so in this area I am self-taught. After finishing my studies I immediately started freelancing, so my professional background in fashion illustration lies in my client list which includes numerous fashion brands and fashion magazines.

- Where do you find your inspiration?

Inspiration comes from anything that triggers my nerve to create, that could be anything really, an unusual color combination, an interesting face etc., and of course I buy a lot of books and magazines, visits galleries, go shopping for oddities, and search the Internet and other common places for inspiration. I also take a lot of inspiration from fashion photography and models that have a look I am drawn to.

- In terms of creation techniques, in which aspect do you think you distinguish from other fashion illustrators?

I think I am quite broad in my use of techniques and style. This can work against you in the sense that your style is perhaps not always instantly recognizable, and as an artist, instant recognition is of course a good thing. However, I love the experimental part of creating, and exploring is an integral ingredient in my work. Also, being broad can be an advantage as it can open up to a wider market for commissions.

- What do you think of the current forms of expression for fashion illustration?

I love how fashion illustration seems to be seeing a revival in the more traditional sense. Social media has also opened up so we can discover not only the ones that are published, but anyone who loves fashion illustration and wants to share what he or she does.

Julia Seeman/Refinery 29 2015

1
Bottega Veneta SS16/Show Studio
2
Part of the "New Nordic Fashion Illustration Vol.2" Exhibition

1 | 2
　 | 3

1
Personal 2015
2
Personal 2015
3
Vogue Nippon/Prada SS16

067

1 2 | 4
3

1
Personal 2014
2
Personal 2014
3
Alberta Ferretti SS16/Show Studio
4
"Gina" Personal 2015

Raphaël Vicenzi

Raphaël Vicenzi, a.k.a "Mydeadpony," is a self-taught Belgian artist and illustrator who lives in Brussels, Belgium. His illustration and watercolor techniques are influenced by fashion, street art and graffiti, and inspired by female beauty. By mixing digital media with painting and sketches and drawing on top of watercolors, splotches and textures, he creates immensely detailed images that are both meticulous and ethereal.

Tools and materials: Photoshop, collage of watercolors and mixed textures

■ How did you get in touch with fashion illustration?

I have always really liked fashion illustration in general but it was more of a happenstance to work in this field than a well-thought-out plan or career goal.

■ Where do you find your inspiration?

I keep a note book with different ideas or personal thoughts but most of the real work begins when all those influences are coming up subconsciously when I am working on an illustration. My works are more the result of experimentation, happy mistakes and letting subconscious associations rise to the surface of my consciousness than a carefully laid-out plan. Through illustration or collage I try to find a mental place where each new work is an open door to emotions, feelings and moods. My process is quite fluid but I usually build an image layer by layer in Photoshop, either by drawing it or finding the right photo to lay the foundations of the whole image. Then I will be adding textures, elements, cutting pieces, juxtaposing things and sometimes words as I go along. I usually try out different ideas and compositions until I start to get a sense of the meaning of the artwork. Ideas are coming while I am working on a piece, gathering shapes, forms and color. I am merely trying to fit those elements together until they start to talk to me, making connections where there were none before. Sometimes it can be a frustrating process, where nothing seems to make sense and everything is awkward and unbalanced. I enjoy the process of working on a piece as much as the outcome. Each completed work is an invitation for a new creation, different from the last but always sharing the common internal landscape and language where they originate from.

■ In terms of creation techniques, in which aspect do you think you distinguish from other fashion illustrators?

Perhaps in the personal way I incorporate different influences that are not strictly relevant to fashion illustration in general. I don't think I am that different from any other artists, I just try to improve and find new exciting ways to create and hope that people will like my works as well.

■ What do you think of the current forms of expression for fashion illustration? For future creations, in which aspect do you expect to make breakthroughs?

I am not sure to be honest. Personally I'd like to keep working on making short gifs or videos but that's more out of a desire to experiment and learn new things than to make a breakthrough.

1 Ghost Harbour

1
Pilot of the Void
2
21 Juin Web

1 London
2 You Want Me to Disappear

1
6par4 Christine and the Queens
2
Marie Claire Astro Taureau

Shinn Wen

Shinn Wen, Chinese fashion illustrator, graduated from the Academy of Arts & Design of Tsinghua University with a Master's Degree in Fashion Design. She now works in the fashion design faculty of Hubei Institute of Fine Arts, both as an instructor for students and a researcher in ladies' fashion design and illustration. Under the account name of ruthless_wen, she has published her own works on Instagram since 2013 and has established successful business relationships with leading international fashion brands and magazines.

Tools and materials: Liquid, tubular and semi-dry watercolors, miscellaneous waterproof or water-based ink, CANSON watercolor drawing paper, watercolor drawing brush and traditional Chinese writing brush

■ What's the concept of your art creation?

Ever since I was a child, I have entertained an inner love for those beautiful things related to fashion and wished to record them with my pen as an expression of the aesthetics they bring to me. I draw a great deal from classic fashion illustration works in history, and sometimes I aspire to recapture the timeless and concise styles in my own works.

■ Who is your most admired fashion artist?

The artist I admire the most is the American illustrator, Tony Viramontes, who sadly passed away in his prime at the age of 28. From his paintings, I can sense how he depended solely on his flair and subjective sentiments to depict the picture. Each illustration captures a most amazing moment with strong and vigorous lines, captivating his audience.

■ How do you understand the combination of these two fields – fashion and illustration art?

Fashion brings out a diversity of styles and colors in expressive ways; these traits can also be ascribed to illustration artists. Their combination is a natural development as both fashion and illustration produce distinct impressions of the times.

■ How does the knowledge of fashion effect your illustration art?

The advantage is the ability for artists to instill more of their personal elements, incorporate their own interpretation of fashion and reveal the style of those fashion products with unconventional and bolder ways while creatively integrating a myriad of otherwise irrelevant elements into original, unique and novel pictures.

1
Apartment Building

1
Far Out Far 01

1
Far Out Far 02
2
Greet Fleet 01
3
Far Out Far 03

1 | 2

1
Far Out Far 04
2
Greet Fleet 02

David Despau

David Despau began his university studies in Architecture but eventually graduated as a Fine Arts major specializing in Design. Since then he has freelanced in the world of design and advertising, and held positions as Art Director and Creative Director at several digital advertising agencies. He has worked for prestigious magazines such as *Time*, *The New Yorker*, *ESPN* magazine, *Car & Driver*, etc. and for commercial clients such as Porsche, Kinder, Burton, DC comics, Warner Bros and Coty France, just to name a few. Recently he has been recognized in the prestigious Taschen's publication *100 Illustrators* as one of the most influential international illustrators of the last decade. Other works have also been published in books such as *Illustration Now* (Taschen) featuring his illustration on the 3rd edition cover, *The New Age of Feminine Drawing* (Allrightsreserved), *Illusive 3* (Gestalten), *200 Best illustrators* (Luezers) and *Portraits* (Taschen), among others.

Tools and materials: Ballpoint pen, ink, watercolor, pen and photoshop

■ How did you get in touch with fashion illustration?

I started illustrating professionally because "fashion illustration" was trending in my country and there were a lot of great illustrators doing this kind of illustration. They inspired me.

■ Where do you find your inspiration?

Inspirations come from my surroundings: art, music, fashion, photography, social networks, blogs, films… everything that enters through my eyes is an inspiration.

■ In terms of creation techniques, in which aspect do you think you distinguish from other fashion illustrators?

Maybe it's the use of traditional and technological techniques being mixed together and the unfinished result of my work. As Steven Heller said of my work, "David Despau creates exquisite portraits, elegant yet modest. The illusionist-like precision and most 'photographic' quality highlights the personality of those portrayed. The contemporary quality of his work is in the infinite details balanced by space, so that what is carefully excluded says as much as what is so precisely included."

■ What do you think of the current forms of expression for fashion illustration? For future creations, in which aspect do you expect to make breakthroughs?

I don't think it's restricted to fashion illustration but it's the same for all kinds of illustrations. There have always been trends in illustration: traditional techniques, computer, minimalism, flat colors, collage, textures, etc., but I think creating relevant, inspiring, and impactful illustrations that evoke emotions will always be a trend. And I am always looking for new inspirations.

1
CHICO Glasses

1
Yellow 02
2
HER

1
HIM
2
Yorokobu
3
RA_CHICA_OK 02

1 2 4
3

1 Rachel
2 Morena
3 Ella
4 Girl Tattoo

Gabriel Villena

Born in Santiago, Chile, Gabriel Villena studied graphic design and art and worked for various advertising agencies, publishers and on projects that interested her. In recent years she has focused her dedication on illustration, developing her passion for drawing and fashion. Gabriel's works have been presented in art magazines, books and on television sets and exhibitions. Inspired by the study, work and research surrounding a garment or collection, Gabriel feels fashion illustration reflects a certain time, lifestyle and emotions in its pursuit of beauty.

Tools and materials: Adobe Photoshop, pencil, watercolor and pastel

▪ What's the concept of your art creation?

The process that leads to my design concept is highly influenced by my surroundings and the arts in general: film, theater, illustrations, paintings, fashion designers, musicians, writers and photography. I look for images that inspire me, especially those from the 1920s, 30's and later the 70's. I also seek out attractive poses, looking to capture figures that display ambiguity and are light and fluent. My work is a mix of modern and traditional techniques, along with design and art, but without a very structured idea. I only use digital media as a tool to complement and capture an idea. Each illustration involves a conceptual reflection of its strength and aesthetic possibilities, then followed by many schematic designs, pencil sketches, then digitizing layering, and editing several times to sharpen the drawing or color. Digital layering can involve stains, textures, watercolor, oil, pastel and line value to enrich the drawing. Throughout this tedious creative process I seek to represent an ideal of personal beauty: delicate, androgynous, silent, ambiguous, decadent, frivolous and stylized.

▪ Who is your most admired fashion artist?

In fashion design I greatly admire the elegance and use of art in YSL (Yves Saint Laurent) designs. I also like Alexander McQueen and his eye for the theatrical. Their designs on the catwalk expanded our view of being fashion-forward and both have been very inspiring. In the field of fashion illustration, the works I admire are that of René Gruau, Bouche, Antonio and Eric, and also David Downton, who revived fashion illustration in an era saturated by pictures.

▪ How do you understand the combination of these two fields – fashion and illustration art?

The collaboration between fashion and illustration has always existed, in fact the latter was for a long time the only way to communicate fashion. Both are still widely used together but I am more interested in the personal vision proposed by the illustrator to show the work of a designer: technology and talent combined to enhance a garment.

▪ What do you think about the advantage of fashion design in the form of illustration?

In my view, fashion design is the culmination of photography and illustration, photography being the closest to advertising and illustration to art. When combined they create various elements and languages. Illustration, because of its proximity to art and abundance of current techniques, gives a new dimension and position to fashion in a more aesthetic context.

1
Blue

| 1 | 2 | 3 | 4 |

1 Spring
2 Green
3 Swan
4 Rouge

Ëlodie

With her own realistic and poetic style, Ëlodie has worked in Paris as an illustrator since 2010. Although she prefers using traditional techniques, she enjoys experimenting with new ones to infuse more soul into her illustrations. Ëlodie is fascinated by fashion and also often gets inspiration from the nostalgic universe of her childhood.

Tools and materials: Pencil, watercolor and Adobe Photoshop

- How did you get in touch with fashion illustration?

For as long as I can remember I have always been drawing or creating. In my childhood, and till today, I am always fascinated by Disney's movies and my first dream was to become a cartoon animator. But after three years of working in the animation industry, I felt that there was something missing. My creativity was restrained by agencies' requests. So one day I just quit my job and started to work as an independent illustrator. I received my first commissions in the beginning of 2010 and then joined Colagene in 2011. The moment my career as a fashion illustrator started was when I received my first important orders in advertising from Colagene.

- Where do you find your inspiration?

My inspiration comes from everywhere, but mainly fashion. I also have a fascination for everything from the 1960s. And living in Paris influences a lot my work as I have started drawing a lot of Parisian girls and buildings recently.

- In terms of creation techniques, in which aspect do you think you distinguish from other fashion illustrators?

Maybe my uniqueness lies in the fact that all of my drawings are entirely drawn by hand, before being digitally colorized... I think this process helps to inject a bit of poetry and soul into my illustrations.

- What do you think of the current forms of expression for fashion illustration? For future creations, in which aspect do you expect to make breakthroughs?

I love seeing the evolution of fashion illustration and I'm inspired by illustrators from both the 20th century and today. In the future I think that I will add more abstract qualities and textures in my illustrations in order to create something unconventional yet impactful.

1

1
Glamour Espana_mois

1
Lazy Girls

1
Gorgeous

2
La Marelle

1
121115_RA_La_Marelle_eelodie_carte_02
2
121126_Elodie_vogue

Katrinn Pelletier

Katrinn Pelletier lives in Quebec City, Canada, with her partner and their two cats. Living right in the heart of the old town, UNESCO's Historic District of Old Québec, Katrinn draws inspiration from the area surrounded by the St. Laurent River. Influenced by urban life and fashion, she creates sensitive and poetic images on tracing paper with spots made of ink or watercolor, which are then integrated into precise lines, a process that gives life to characters. Katrinn has a keen interest in the aesthetics of the 1950's, and is also inspired by vintage objects giving a refreshing touch to her work. Her work has been awarded on many occasions by the LUX Awards (Quebec) and Applied Arts Awards (Canada).

Tools and materials: Pencil, watercolor and Adobe Photoshop

- **How did you get in touch with fashion illustration?**

I was trained in visual arts and graphic design. I think all art forms are connected to each other and are inspired by and affect each other. I was attracted to fashion art, color and texture. For me, fashion is a means of expression with many possibilities. It lets us know who we are and who we want to be, or what we don't want to be.

- **Where do you find your inspiration?**

I find inspiration in daily life, including the light, color, texture, object, person, or a character. I'm interested in the art on the streets, what people do with what they choose to wear, buy and how they relate and express themselves. I like things that have a story, a soul, the old mixed with the new. In my spare time, I like to travel and discover the relationship of all kinds of objects, clothes and old vintage photographs or illustrations.

- **In terms of creative techniques, in which aspect do you think you distinguish yourself from other fashion illustrators?**

There are so many talented artists and illustrators in the world, and I don't pretend to be one. My images are digital, and I work with a variety of textures that I create, using spots of watercolor and pencil strokes that, I think, is something personal for my illustrations.

- **What do you think of the current forms of expression for fashion illustration? For future creations, in which aspect do you expect to make breakthroughs?**

Globalization, new technologies and Internet have democratized professional illustrators and given rise to a rich amount of talent, and that is good news. The most interesting change, in my opinion, is that they have given a soul to their images: a personal touch. As for my part, in the future, I'd like to have the opportunity to work with a designer and fashion designer on a product or textiles, or an advertising campaign. You never know what life could bring to an illustrator, and I love it!

1
Printemps.4

1 Beach Summer
2 Printemps.2
3 Printemps.5

1		5	6
2	3 4	7	

1
Bouquet
2
Mintshoes.2015
3
Escarpin.plume
4
Gougoune.plume
5
Mars.promo
6
Plume.Face
7
Printemps.3

1
Marie Claire China

Lutheen

Lutheen is a 32-year-old French illustrator who has worked as a freelancer for press, textile, edition, advertising and decoration companies during the past six years.

Tools and materials: Watercolor, ink and pen

- What's the concept of your art creation?

My universe is poetic, sweetened, and colored. I am inspired by fashion, nature, decoration and by Provence's spirit. I try to re-transcribe a sensitive and soft world.

- Who is your most admired fashion artist?

I admire Hugo Pratt and Gustav Klimt the most.

- What do you think about the advantage of fashion design in the form of illustration?

Everything is possible in drawing where dreams transcend into reality.

- In terms of creation techniques, in which aspect do you think you distinguish from other fashion illustrators?

I follow French fashion trends according to my own taste. I like simplicity, natural looks, and the bohemian style. I try to add the natural feeling into my illustrations, which is accentuated by the feminine hairstyles and the natural movement of hair. I like accessories and printed matters. I always work in a traditional way and have never drawn on a computer. To compose a better image, I draw all the elements of my illustrations separately and assemble them with a computer, thus I can return to an image again and again until she pleases me perfectly.

1
Chamane

| 1 | 2 |
| | 3 |

1
05 Sept
2
Fille Maillot Glace
3
Fille Couronne Fleur

Look by Kutch & Couture

SAN MARINA

Look by Sophie la Modeuse

SAN MARINA

| 1 | 4 |
| 2 3 | |

1
Illu-Achrome
2
San Marina K&C
3
San Marina Modeuse
4
Love Compagnie

Ko. Machiyama

Ko. Machiyama is based in Tokyo, and belongs to "BUILDING" and "Professional Illustrators Group ILLUSTRATORS TSUSHIN". Ko. Machiyama produces illustrations with movement, shape, and space as the theme. His work is dignified, quiet and reminiscent, making the viewer recollect the story.

Tools and materials: Pencil, paper, acrylic paint, color ink, iMac and Photoshop

- How did you get in touch with fashion illustration?

  I was interested in fashion, so I learned textile design at university.

- Who is your most admired fashion artist?

  David Townton.

- How do you understand the combination of these two fields – fashion and illustration art?

  They are good for each other.

- What do you think about the advantage of fashion design in the form of illustration?

  Illustration can demonstrate more clearly the concepts and images of fashion.

1
Textile Design

1
Greeting Card 2016 (The Year of Monkey)
2
Honor of Spring

1 2 3
4   *5 6*

1
Hermes, MilkX
2
Sacai, MilkX
3
Marni, MilkX
4
Loewe, MilkX
5
Umit Benan, MilkX
6
Saint Laurant, MilkX

Mamzelle Poppy

As a lover for color, fabric and other materials, Mamzelle Poppy has found her own way to express herself through illustration for several years now. After Mamzelle finished the 3D digital training (specialized in texture adding), her graphic tablet became her best ally. Her work is made up of different elements, creating a pop, graphic and colored aesthetic. She seeks out the beauty in everything, and then transposes it into her personal universe with a suspicion of naughtiness and whim. This universe reflects a very personal vision of femininity. Mamzelle's approach is mostly intuitive: she approaches her creations with feeling and makes the most of her best tool: creativity.

Tools and materials: Photoshop and graphics tablets

- How did you get in touch with fashion illustration?

I discovered fashion illustration during my studies in computer graphics animation. I was a fan of artists like Esra Roise, Conrad Roset and Paula Bonet and gradually I started to create my own vision in order to follow those that I admire, and with time my own style started to emerge. I have no direct experience related to fashion illustration; I learned everything I know by myself. But I know I've always had a fashion sensibility and a strong passion for this very creative field, and I do follow the day-to-day fashion.

- Where do you find your inspiration?

I get inspired by all artistic forms and images: photography, art, films, animated movies, fabrics and objects, and also by cartoon films. I seek out the beauty in everything and then transpose it into my personal universe.

- In terms of creation techniques, in which aspect do you think you distinguish from other fashion illustrators?

My work can be distinguished from others graphically as it is primarily digital, bold and very colorful. Added textures and materials are a little plus in my works.

- What do you think of the current forms of expression for fashion illustration? For future creations, in which aspect do you expect to make breakthroughs?

Styles are very different. I think there are as many styles as there are artists, but the predominant technique is the classic drawing technique, by hand. Today digital art is the center of all media, so I think that digital technology can meet the challenges in many future creations, and I will explore more of those mediums in the future and in my work approach.

1 Taurus Girl Horoscope Version

1
Alex Portrait
2
Flamingo Girl

```
1 2    4 5
  3
```

1
Iris Apfel
2
San Marina K&C
3
Pierrot
4
Porter Girl
5
The Photographer

Natalia Sanabria

Natalia Sanabria was born and still resides in San José, Costa Rica. She has always loved fashion magazines as they were her first introduction to fashion illustrations and her realization of wanting to draw for a living. She took many art courses while growing up and continued her endeavor at the University of Costa Rica where she graduated with a bachelor's degree in Graphic Design and Painting. Working as a graphic designer by day and drawing in her free time she realized her passion for illustration. The passion was too strong to ignore, so she decided to give up her graphic design position to work as a freelance illustrator.

Tools and materials: Watercolor, pencils and collage

▪ What's the concept of your art creation?

As a lover for colors and patterns, I define my work as expressive, detail-oriented. I always use pencils and mix them during the process with watercolor, which blends very well. My main themes are backstage fashion moments and models on the runway, for in a way drawing them makes me feel like being part of the show. But what I enjoy the most is drawing hair and faces with bold make-up.

▪ Who is your most admired fashion artist?

Some of my favorite painters are Gustav Klimt, Degas and Toulouse-Lautrec. They influenced me by their particular styles and the dramatic women they portrayed. In fashion my all-time favorite designer would be Meadham Kirchhoff. Every collection is very appealing to me and I have found a huge satisfaction in drawing their collections. Their aesthetic is so creative, unlike anything I've ever seen in fashion.

▪ How do you understand the combination of these two fields – fashion and illustration art?

I think that fashion has always gone hand-in-hand with illustration, before there is photography illustrators were documenting fashion in an informative but beautiful way. And for a designer an idea always starts with a sketch.

▪ What do you think about the advantage of fashion design in the form of illustration?

The advantage of fashion design in the form of illustration is that, today with all the technology and digital photos everywhere, it is refreshing to see illustrators and designers take notice and share fan art on different social media outlets.

1
Pretty in Pink
2
On the Run
3
Bows

1
Dior
2
Girls Girls Girls

1 2 | 3 4

1
Marco Viscenzo
2
Rodarte
3
Elizabeth
4
Charles Jeffrey

Nicole Jarecz

Nicole Jarecz's journey as an illustrator began when she graduated from the College for Creative Studies in Detroit, Michigan in 2010 with a BFA in Illustration. The real adventure started when she moved to Paris, France where she lived and worked for six years as a fashion illustrator. She is now one of the 35 artists worldwide who initiated Colagene Creative Clinic. Her delicate and feminine illustrations are a result of playing with graphite, ink, watercolor and textures digitally. Striving to find a balance between being playful and detailed in her work by combining traditional and digital methods, she finds inspiration in everyday events, fashion, travel, watching people and living in Paris, France.

Tools and materials: Graphite, ink, watercolor and digital software

■ How did you get in touch with fashion illustration?

I became interested in fashion illustration during my junior year at the College for Creative Studies. I worked with my professor and now mentor, Don Kilpatrick, to explore different techniques that applied to fashion illustration. I have now been working in the field of fashion illustration since 2010. I've had the privilege of working with many clients in the fashion world such as *Elle Girl* magazine, *Glamour* magazine, *Marie Claire*, *Madame Figaro* and *Commons & Sense* to name a few.

■ Where do you find your inspiration?

I found so much inspiration from living in Paris. I lived in Paris for six years as a fashion illustrator. Paris is really the center of fashion. There is life and beauty around every corner. You can do people watching all day while enjoying the best food in the world on a terrace that is over 100 years old. History, culture, and cuisine in a city that never sleeps – this is inspiration at its best.

■ In terms of creation techniques, in which aspect do you think you distinguish from other fashion illustrators?

It's all about a feeling and an attention to detail. I'm very detailed in my work and strive to have a realistic aspect to my work like that of a photograph. I like it when the face is very realistic but the forms around are loose and gestural. There is something unique about pieces that can't be taken with a camera. I'm a big fan of mixing traditional and digital techniques. I think many illustrations lean one way or the other but I like their combination during my work.

■ What do you think of the current forms of expression for fashion illustration? For future creations, in which aspect do you expect to make breakthroughs?

I think that today there are many very talented fashion illustrators out there who all have different styles. This is what makes fashion illustration so exciting because it's ever evolving. I think it's important for a fashion illustrator to experiment with new techniques even if it's only through your sketchbook. It may lead to a new style that you may apply to your work. I hope to continue to evolve in the years to come!

1 Couture
2 Flower Dress

1
Dior Dresses
2
Dior Dress

1
Commons & Sense 01
2
Commons & Sense 04
3
Ralph Lauren

Sandra Suy

Born and currently living in Barcelona, Sandra Suy has chosen drawing as a way to best express herself. After completing fashion design studies in Barcelona, she first worked in graphic design and later moved on to designing prints for clothing brands. This re-encounter of fashion with the drawing world encouraged the start of her own career as a fashion illustrator, linking her two passions.

Tools and materials: Mixed techniques

- How do you summarize the characteristics of your work?

I like to express the maximum using minimal elements and colors. I think the strength is in the details. I like to play with textures, overlays and patterns, creating the collage effect.

- Who is your most admired fashion artist?

Some of my favourites are René Gruau and Egon Schielle, among others.

- How do you understand the combination of these two fields – fashion and illustration art?

I think fashion and illustration complement each other well because both speak about beauty and creativity.

- What do you think about the advantage of fashion design in the form of illustration?

Fashion is a great source of inspiration for an illustrator. And fashion illustration emphasizes and gives prominence to the artistic side of fashion.

1

1
McQueen

1	2	4
3		

1
Martha Stewart/Vneck
2
Martha Stewart/A Line
3
Piscis
4
55DSL

1 Adrienne
2 Capricorn/Glamour UK

Silke Werzinger

Silke Werzinger is a freelance illustrator in Berlin, Germany. Her simple style, which combines ink and color, has an almost adolescent brazenness, and her illustrations tell amusing stories in scenes taken from everyday life, like conversations between friends, fashion and music. She has illustrated several books and has worked for various clients such as Condé Nast, L'Oréal, Daimler, NYLON, Marie Claire and *Cosmopolitan* magazine and is represented by Colagene Creative Clinic.

Tools and materials: Pencil, ballpoint pen, ink, watercolor and Photoshop

- How did you get in touch with fashion illustration?

I studied communication design with a focus on illustration. During my studies I spent half a year interning in different studios of some great fashion illustrators and they helped me out with all the questions a student would have. I also have a strong interest in fashion, fashion photography and pop culture and my illustration style is an expression of things and styles I find interesting.

- Where do you find your inspiration?

I find inspiration in everyday life, magazines, notebooks I pick up at flea markets, and people photography. I also find beauty in imperfect things.

- In terms of creation techniques, in which aspect do you think you distinguish from other fashion illustrators?

I think this is a question potential clients have to answer.

- What do you think of the current forms of expression for fashion illustration? For future creations, in which aspect do you expect to make breakthroughs?

There is a great diversity in illustration, which I love. I don't consciously think about evolving my style, because it happens naturally with a change of perspective and interest.

1

1
Votre Beaute

1
Mavi Berlin

2
NOVA Concept Campaign

1 Gemini
2 Aries

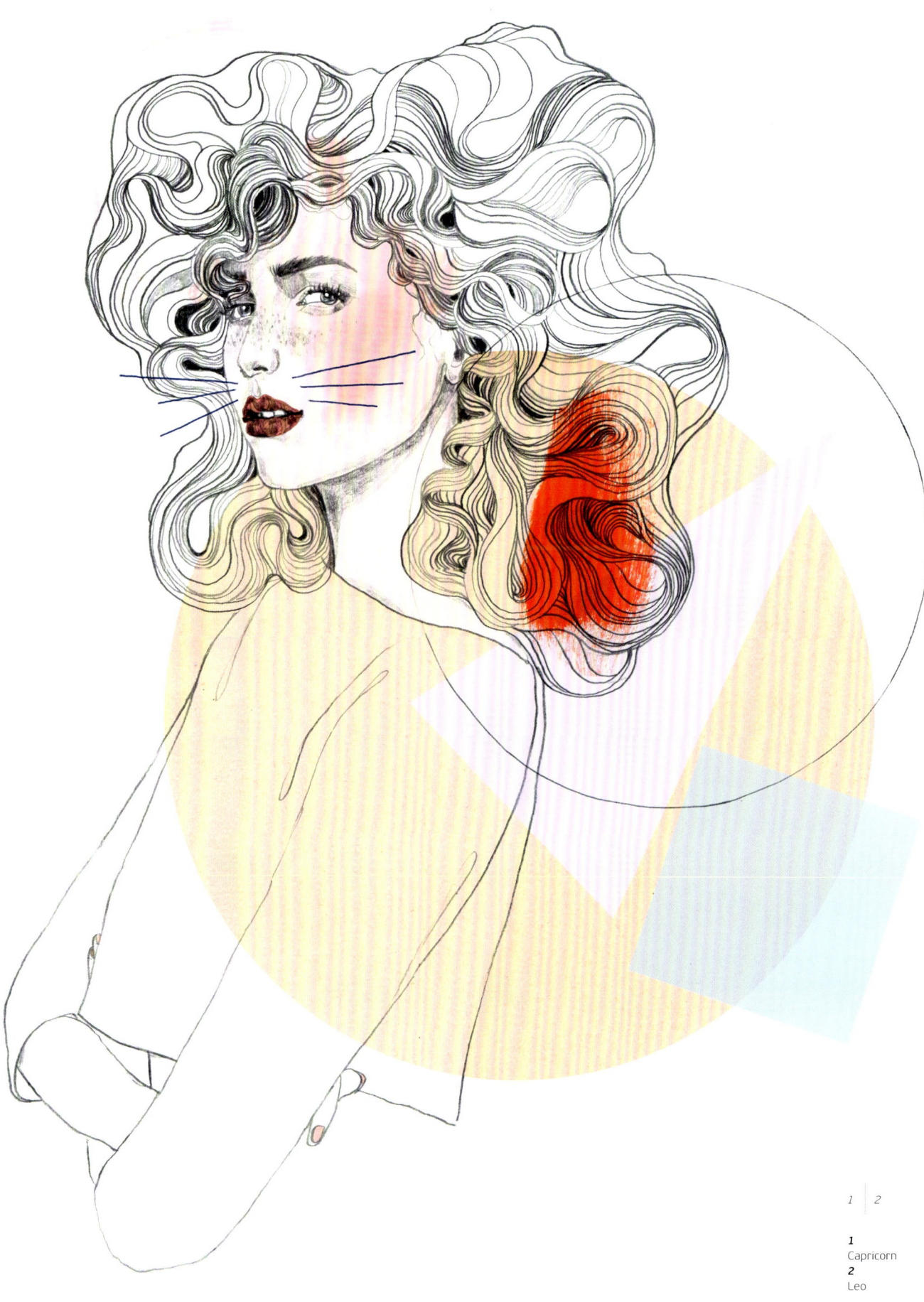

1 | 2

1 Capricorn
2 Leo

1
Medusa 01
2
Cover of *Enorm* Magazine

1
Sunglass Hut
2
Undone

Stina Persson

Stina Persson uses ink, watercolor and collages to create a style that is both vivid and elegant. She fuses the traditional with the cutting-edge to introduce a modern look – a look that is appreciated by numerous clients including Nike, Microsoft, Louis Vuitton, Veuve Clicquot, L'Oreal, O.P.I., *Vogue Japan*, *W* magazine, and *WWD* magazine. Stina studied fine art in Perugia, fashion drawing in Florence, and has a degree in illustration from Pratt Institute in New York. She was awarded the Society of Illustrator's Student Scholarship in 1996 & 1997, and has exhibited her work in several shows in New York and Japan.

Tools and materials: Ink, watercolor and collage

- Who is your most admired fashion artist?

Fashion designer – Miuccia Prada, she inspires me every time, and fashion illustrator – Rene Gruau.

- Where do you find your inspiration?

I find inspiration in nature, on the streets, and in books and magazines. While working, I listen to Podcasts and music, and drink good coffee or Earl Gray tea.

- How do you understand the combination of these two fields – fashion and illustration art?

As fashion photography take over in the 60's, fashion illustration played a new role in the 90's, no longer showing fabrics and hemlines, but capturing the feeling of the person wearing the garment.

- In terms of creation techniques, in which aspect do you think you distinguish from other illustrators?

The use of lots of paper and less digital technique than most people, I would think. I don't have a special figure that I create again and again, but I also want each image to have its own personality.

1
Prada Brunette 03

	3	5
1		
2	4	

1 Dance
2 Dress
3 Prada FW2010
4 Big Bow
5 Chloe Gold

1
Fake Leopard Coat
2
Le Kid
3
Dancer 02
4
Dancer

1 Skin
2 Tomford

Svetlana Makarova

A Ukrainian self-taught fashion illustrator, Svetlana Makarova has always been fond of art and fashion, letting her passion lead the way. Her illustrations focus on creating appealing and accomplished looks for exquisite fashion characters that tell little stories or just strike poses. Paying attention to details, shapes, volume, lighting, and textures of fabrics, Svetlana uses fresh vibrant colors and a bit of humor in her creation.

Tools and materials: Adobe Illustrator, Wacom Intuos3 A4 and Adobe Photoshop

■ What's the concept of your art creation?

In my illustrations I aim to show the impact a particular fashion look had on me, and usually this ends up as a story, or maybe even a fashion fairy tale. The medium I'm using currently for my art is vector. Every piece is a new challenge for me, for example, I would set new goals to achieve, try to work with complex shapes and many patterns, or I would want to create a specific atmosphere. Being able to express my thoughts, feelings or just telling some funny little story with my art, and growing professionally with every piece, is a great pleasure for me and an essential part of my life.

■ Who is your most admired fashion artist?

I have a lot of favorite fashion illustrators, but at the moment they are: Roberto Sánchez – I love his unique geometric style; Mahyar M.Kalantari – his dark and exquisite illustrations simply take my breath away; Sunny Gu – her bright playful girls always amaze me; David Downton and René Gruau – I like their clean style, classical fashion illustration.

■ How do you understand the combination of these two fields – fashion and illustration art?

These two together have become a new trend – fashion illustration art. As the word art implies, it incorporates more artistic techniques than illustrations do.

■ What do you think about the advantage of fashion design in the form of illustration?

Fashion illustration has no limits in what can be illustrated and is very unique to the person illustrating, because only one artist works on the illustration, showing their unique view on expressing fashion and emotion, while fashion photography is a product of a group of professionals.

1
Valentino Red Pre-fall2015

1
Lanvin Fall RTW2015
2
Givenchy SS2015
3
Alberta Ferretti RTW Fall 2014
4
THEO SS16

1
Comme des Garcons: The Fire Queen
2
New Old Tales – Grow Up Alice, McQueen D&G FW2014
3
New Old Tales – Snow Queen Maleficent, McQueen D&G FW2014

| 1 | 3 |
| 2 | |

1
Valentino MIME Bag
2
New Old Tales – Red Riding Hood
Snowhite, McQueen D&G FW2014
3
Flapper

Yana Moskaluk

Yana Moskaluk was born and raised in Omsk, Siberia. Since childhood she has been interested in drawing and studied art and design in Omsk. At the age of 19 she moved to Moscow, where she was invited to work in the most popular Russian design studio, Art. Lebedev, as an illustrator. Her illustrations were used in magazines, books, CD covers, posters, advertising and logos in many countries. Yana's works have also been featured in art exhibitions in Russia, Switzerland, the United States and Poland. The first strong art impression for her was Russian artist Mikhail Vrubel. Myths, legends and fairy tales became the main subject for her artworks and Yana tries to catch the magical dark atmosphere while keeping her look fresh and modern.

Tools and materials: Adobe Illustrator and Photoshop

- How do you summarize the characteristics of your work?

Fashion inspires me and I like including some elements of it in my works. I often use historical garments and ornaments, giving them a modern look, helping to create the atmosphere I need.

- Who is your most admired fashion artist?

I like illustrations of theatrical costume designs by Leon Bakst.

- How do you understand the combination of these two fields – fashion and illustration art?

I love illustration and fashion and I think combining these two gives us a new form of art. The way an illustrator draws makes each fashion piece unique.

- What do you think of the current forms of expression for fashion illustration?

New technologies are everything today. New formats, animation, 3D, all of these things let fashion illustration be bold and modern. I think new materials are great and move art to the next level.

1

1
The Diamond Chariot

1
Spring
2
Koschei the Immortal

1 Hydra
2 Night
3 The Frog Princess

1 Cinderella
2 Elysia

NEW FASHION ILLUSTRATION

Author: Dopress Books
Commissioning Editors: Guo Guang, Mang Yu
                      Chen Hao, Zeng Sheng
English Editors: Jenny Qiu, Dora Ding
Copy Editor: Anne Bethany
Book Designer: Qiu Hong

©2016 by China Youth Press, Roaring Lion Media Co., Ltd. and CYP International Ltd. China Youth Press, Roaring Lion Media Co., Ltd. and CYP International Ltd. have all rights which have been granted to CYP International Ltd. to publish and distribute the English edition globally.

First published in the United Kingdom in 2016 by CYPI PRESS

Add: 79 College Road, Harrow Middlesex, HA1 1BD, UK
Tel: +44 (0) 20 3178 7279
E-mail: sales@cypi.net editor@cypi.net
Website: www.cypi.net
ISBN: 978-1-908175-77-9
Printed in China